"It has been 500 years since Martin Luther triggered the protestant reformation. Yet, his work has rarely been mined for its implications on ministry with children and youth. Todd Hobart offers a creative and insightful look into how Luther's theology and practice influenced the work with children and youth in the church, society, and the home. This is a timely addition to both the field of youth ministry and Luther studies."

—**Jeremy Myers**
PhD, AiM, Religion Department, Youth and Family Ministry,
Augsburg College

"For congregations rooted in the Reformation and seeking new understandings of faith formation, *Martin Luther as Youth Worker* is worth a look. Grounded in history with an eye to the present, this book brings readers into Luther's life and asks questions that are real today. What is our calling as parents? What is society's role in preparing the next generation? How is faith formed? How do the absurdities of the Christian faith translate into our actions in society? Short and easy to read, Hobart's work is fitting for a variety of people—youth workers, parents, educators, and congregational leaders seeking to rethink forming faith. I highly recommend it."

—**Terri Martinson Elton**
Associate Professor of Leadership, Luther Seminary, St. Paul, MN

Martin Luther
as
Youth Worker

Martin Luther as Youth Worker

Insights from the Great Reformer
for Modern Youth and Children's Ministry

Todd Hobart

◆PICKWICK *Publications* · Eugene, Oregon

MARTIN LUTHER AS YOUTH WORKER
Insights from the Great Reformer for Modern Youth and Children's Ministry

Copyright © 2017 Todd Hobart. All rights reserved. Except for brief quotations in critical publications or reviews, no part of this book may be reproduced in any manner without prior written permission from the publisher. Write: Permissions, Wipf and Stock Publishers, 199 W. 8th Ave., Suite 3, Eugene, OR 97401.

Pickwick Publications
An Imprint of Wipf and Stock Publishers
199 W. 8th Ave., Suite 3
Eugene, OR 97401

www.wipfandstock.com

PAPERBACK ISBN: 978-1-4982-9027-2
HARDCOVER ISBN: 978-1-4982-9029-6
EBOOK ISBN: 978-1-4982-9028-9

Cataloging-in-Publication data:

Names: Hobart, Todd, author.
Title: Martin Luther as youth worker : insights from the great reformer for modern youth and children's ministry / Todd Hobart.
Description: Eugene, OR: Pickwick Publications, 2017 | Includes bibliographical references.
Identifiers: ISBN: 978-1-4982-9027-2 (paperback). | ISBN: 978-1-4982-9029-6 (hardcover). | ISBN: 978-1-4982-9028-9 (ebook).
Subjects: Luther, Martin, 1483–1546 | Church work with youth.
Classification: BR334.3 H62 2017 (paperback) | BR334.3 (ebook)

Manufactured in the U.S.A.   03/13/17

Contents

Abbreviations | vii
Preface | ix

1 Martin Luther's Care for Children and Youth | 1
2 Luther and Education | 13
3 Luther and Faith Formation | 33
4 Luther and Reason | 52
5 Conclusion | 69

Bibliography | 73

Abbreviations

WA Weimar Ausgabe (Weimar edition of Luther's works)

TR *Tischreden* (Table Talk) in WA

Preface

"And why do old people live, except to care for, teach,
and bring up the young?"[1]

—Martin Luther

On October 31, 1517, a young Augustinian monk named Martin Luther nailed his ninety-five theses to the door of All Saints' Church in Wittenberg, Germany, thus igniting the Protestant Reformation that would sweep the Western world. This Reformation brought not only religious and theological innovations but also institutional change to the Roman Catholic church, political change to the Holy Roman Empire and other countries of Europe, and it set the stage for the profound philosophical changes of modernity and the Enlightenment.

This is the story that is told in classrooms everywhere—in high schools, colleges, and seminaries alike. In this book, however, I'd like to take a look at a less explored

---

1. From his *Letter to the Mayors and Aldermen of all the Cities of Germany in Behalf of Christian Schools,* 1524; quoted in Painter, *Luther on Education,* 177.

Preface

aspect of the great reformer's life: his relationship with and care for children and youth, and, specifically, what this could mean for children, youth, and family ministry today.

I've had a few personal influences that spurred me on to consider this less discussed aspect of Luther's life. First, in my own work with youth in both evangelical and mainline Protestant churches, I have found that youth workers, sadly, seem to be less valued than others who work with adults in churches. Typically, youth workers are younger, less experienced, and are paid much less than other pastors or church staff. The old stereotype always was that the typical duration of employment for a youth worker lasted about eighteen months. Often, youth workers have also made silly or immature mistakes; I've had some experience with that as well.

I can't speak for all children's ministers, but I suspect many of them could claim similar prejudices against them. The expectation seems to be that one day a youth worker will "graduate" to a higher ministry level and go on to work with adults in some capacity. I know that others in our culture who work with children and youth could have similar issues with their pay and treatment. Whether they are schoolteachers, childcare workers, or after-school program staff, it seems like those who work with children and youth are rarely afforded the respect and esteem of others in our culture.

With this in mind, I was always impressed with what I heard about the care and attention that Luther paid to children and youth. Here was one of the brightest minds and most accomplished theologians in the history of the church, so why would he pay any special attention to the children and youth of his day? Workers with children and youth were certainly not more prized in Luther's time than

Preface

they are today and it seemingly made little sense for this brilliant reformer to value them as he did.

This wondering about Luther and his care for children and youth was further stoked by the publication of Andy Root's book, *Bonhoeffer as Youth Worker*.[2] I was inspired by the idea that one could learn lessons about youth ministry today from great theologians of the past, and that spurred me to take a deeper look at just how Luther cared for children and youth of his day.

The final piece that prompted me to action was the upcoming 500th anniversary of the nailing of the theses to the church door. With the increased attention to Luther and his work that I knew would be coming in 2017, I wanted to make a small contribution to the study of Luther on a subject about which I have great passion.

Before this subject is considered, there are a few caveats to this study that need to be stated. First, as I am not a professional historian. I was humbled nearly every time I opened a book about Luther to see the breadth and depth of research that has been conducted on the man and his thought, and I know that I am still a relative beginner when it comes to learning about the many facets of Luther.

Second, what is about to be attempted here—extrapolating lessons from the life and thought of a medieval man to today—is a difficult and delicate task. The difference between the basic assumptions and life experiences of a person in Germany in the 1500s and the United States in the twenty-first century is astounding. Luther's era was the time of witches, castles, princes, knights, kings, and plagues. Once, Luther cut his leg with a short sword and

---

2. I was inspired by it but did not read it while researching this book, as I wanted the material on Luther to guide the direction of this book independently of the way Root approached Bonhoeffer.

nearly bled to death.[3] One just does not carry around a short sword today! It goes without saying that the advancements in technology, medicine, communication, and transportation today would have astounded and confused a medieval person. Likewise, the time that Luther inhabited is very foreign to us. Yet, I believe that with careful work to avoid overreaching, lessons can be learned from Luther's priorities and passions around children and youth that can be applied today.

To start, Luther's actual practices with children and youth will be considered. This includes Martin and his wife Katie's practical care for their own children (as well as those of their relatives and friends) and Martin's views on games, fun, and the lives of children.

Next, Luther's contributions to the secular and religious system of education of the 1500s will be considered. Luther's care for children and youth extended to all of Germany as he advocated for the reform of the educational system of his day.

Closely related to educational reform was Luther's attention to faith formation, specifically in his creation of the Small and Large Catechisms. The Small Catechism was used in both schools and homes, as Luther attempted to give attention to forming the faith of families in a time when quality spiritual instruction was tough to come by.

Though not specifically addressed to children and youth, Luther's view on human reason is one that can be beneficial to our work with children and youth today. In a time when Christianity seems to have lost the cultural battle to reason and science, Luther's thoughts on the strengths and limitations of human reason are just as relevant today as they were 500 years ago.

3. Lull and Nelson, *Resilient Reformer*, 16.

Preface

Finally, the book will conclude with some thoughts on what it could mean to be a reformer today. How can we appropriate Luther's reforming spirit to address pertinent issues regarding children and youth in our time?

1

Martin Luther's Care for Children and Youth

If a person sticks around long enough in youth ministry, one can see all kinds of fads come and go. Years ago I helped to organize a church middle school winter retreat. It was at a remote camp where we and our gear had to be towed in a giant sled behind a snow grooming machine to get to the camp. It made for quite a memorable entrance into the camp and the weekend that was planned. But what was really unique about that weekend was not so much the talks that were planned or the small group sessions with the students; instead, it was the games. We had devised several games that we thought were perfect for middle school students.

One game was a contest in which student teams vied to see who could spit live crickets the furthest. I don't remember who won, but the sight of live crickets being shot from the mouths of disgusted but eager students is an enduring memory. Later on, we played a game where four people had to see who could down a hamburger, fries, and soft drink the fastest. The twist to this game though, was that we blended all the fast food together, so the students had a delightful mash of hamburger, fries, and pop, all mixed together. The memorable part of that game was watching the students gag and throw up whatever they swallowed into a garbage can, and then go back and try to drink more to see if they could win the game! It's just another reason why middle school students are special.

Of course we didn't realize at the time that live crickets carry diseases and shouldn't be put in the mouths of middle school students. Likewise, it was probably not the best idea to play a game that made students vomit. We played other strange games around that time in youth ministry as well. I haven't led any games like that in years, and I don't really hear about such games in other ministries either. Fads like disgusting games come and go in youth ministry, and there are some predictable reactions to these excesses as well.

Every once in a while, perhaps to counter these dissipations, voices arise clamoring for more depth in youth ministry. "Enough silly games and pizza parties," they might say, "where is the spirituality?" "Why aren't students serving, or being trained as evangelists, or being discipled and growing in their faith?" These voices often head the opposite direction and look suspiciously at the idea of students having fun for the sake of having fun. Some desire to get rid of anything that is not faith-related, while others simply require that a spiritual practice necessarily accompany any kind of fun activity for students.

So what would Luther think about these discussions? How did he relate to and care for the children, youth, and college students that he encountered? Like everything else in imagining Luther's response to modern issues, a wide gulf separates us from that time. Youth ministry, as such, didn't exist, with its history of small groups, pizza parties, and gross games. But I believe that much can be gained from considering Luther's attitudes toward spirituality, the divide between the sacred and the secular, and just how he cared for the children and youth of his day.

I don't want to unfairly characterize Luther. Perhaps he would have loved live crickets and blended happy meals. But I suspect he may have considered those games to be a bit indecent. This shouldn't at all color anyone's view of Luther, though, because he was no prude or killjoy. Reformation historian Preserved Smith details Luther's approval of all "innocent forms of amusement."[1] Luther enjoyed chess, playing cards, the theater, and he recommended outdoor sports as a substitute for drinking for young nobles, as well as dances for youth.[2]

Gerhard Forde wonders that, "Is it not precisely that when man sees by faith that he is intended to live as a creature and not as a God, then he begins for the first time to see the creaturely as something good?"[3] This valuing of the earthly, creaturely existence was characteristic of Luther's theology. He came to despise the monastic attitude that split men and women into separate classes where some were more spiritual and some were more common.

Luther's view of the sacraments shows his valuing of earthly, creaturely existence as well. God does not primarily come to us through extraordinary means, but through the simplicity of ordinary items: water, bread, and wine. It is God's Word and promise, together with those common

---

1. Smith, *Life and Letters of Martin Luther*, 350.
2. Ibid.
3. Forde, *Where God Meets Man*, 57.

earthly items, and the action of washing, giving, and receiving which constitutes the sacrament.[4] Then, "Once all the spiritual pretension is destroyed by simple, earthly washing and by bread and wine we can begin to believe and hear the promise."[5] Luther puts it this way: "The glory of our God is precisely that for our sakes he comes down to the very depths, into human flesh, into the bread, into our mouths, into our heart, our bosom . . ."[6]

So what could this mean for those of us who work with children and youth? Clearly Luther's valuing of children and youth is one worth emulating today. He struck a healthy balance between an emphasis on discipline, education, and play with his own children and with what he advocated for others. Luther was very much against immoral, lawless behavior among children and youth, and he counseled discipline from parents, and obedience toward parents from children.[7] Yet, having grown up in a home and experienced schools where discipline was harsh, or even cruel, Luther also advocated for restraint in discipline. He knew that children would respond best through loving correction rather than abusive outbursts.[8]

In our work with parents, as children's and youth workers, we too can advocate for healthy parenting choices from families in our churches. Programs like "Love and Logic" can be useful for parents who are struggling with how to best discipline their children and provide them with ways to encourage them to make good choices while

4. Ibid., 74–75.
5. Ibid., 75.
6. Fischer, ed., *Luther's Works*, 131.
7. Painter, *Luther on Education*, 115–19.
8. Ibid., 122–24.

also experiencing the natural consequence of their behaviors.[9] The "40 Assets" program can be a good one for raising awareness of community assets that can help children lead healthy lives.[10] In addition to these, there are many other resources that we can provide to aid parents in the care and discipline of their children.

As will be shown, Luther cared for his own family as well as other children and youth in Germany by advocating for their education. He knew that the only way Germany would thrive, people would contribute, and God would be honored was through an educated populace living out their vocations. We too can advocate for a strong educational system in our communities and come alongside and partner with schools to help that dream become a reality.

Just as Luther valued play, fun, and the creaturely aspects of this world, so also can we emphasize these things with our students in our churches. We are not running mini-monasteries, with the goal of protecting children from the world or setting them on a quest to climb their spiritual ladders up to God. Along with worship, service, mission, growing in faith, and building community, we need to remember what our students never tire of reminding us: that we are still creatures of this earth who need to have fun! Perhaps this love of play could permeate all of these activities, but I also don't think it would hurt us to just enjoy fun for the sake of fun and spend a night together eating pizza, watching movies, and enjoying one another's company.

---

9. Love and Logic Institute, "Love and Logic."
10. Search Institute, "Developmental Assets."

MARTIN AND KATIE'S FOSTER CARE

Remembering to have fun is an important aspect of youth ministry, but there is a serious side as well to the practical care that Martin and Katie Luther extended to children and youth in their day. As well as having six children of their own, the Luther's also helped to raise eleven children who were put into their care: "Andreas, Cyriacus, Fabian and George Kaufmann, Elsa and Lena Kaufmann, Hans Polner who had at least two more siblings, Martin Luther from Mansfeld, and Anna Strauss."[11] Seven were nephews and nieces, and four were from a friend of Martin Luther who lost his wife in the plague.[12]

These children and youth came to the Luther's at differing stages in their lives. Some were young, while others were old enough to enroll in college. The Luther's clearly acted as parents and caregivers for these children, providing for them, disciplining them, and taking an active role in determining their marriages and adult lives.[13] Some of them challenged the Luther's parenting abilities, as young adult children will do today, through bouts of drunkenness and choice of romantic partners.[14]

These types of foster arrangements were not uncommon for the time. Martin Luther himself, during his later teen years, stayed with Ursula Cotta, a wealthy woman who helped him with food and gave him a place to stay while he went to school in Eisenach.[15] At ten years old, Katie

---

11. The Luthers' daughters Elizabeth and Magdalena died before reaching adulthood. Kroker, *The Mother of the Reformation*, 144.

12. Bainton, *Women of the Reformation*, 30.

13. Ibid., 145–52.

14. Ibid.

15. Bruce, *Luther as an Educator*, 63.

Luther was placed in a nunnery when her father remarried.[16] According to his description of informal foster care, Harrington states that "most early modern children experienced some form of fostering, whether temporary care for a few days . . . or for several months or even years."[17]

Putting the Luther's care for children in context demands an historical understanding of the challenges of raising children. There were many reasons why children stayed outside the home of biological parents, some for better reasons than others. In the worst cases, often occurring with illegitimate children of poor parents, infants were surreptitiously left to die by neglect, or placed outside to die of exposure.

Among others, Pope Innocent III responded to this problem by supporting foundling hospitals, after witnessing countless infant bodies afloat on the Tiber River.[18] These hospitals would care for infants left behind by their parents, either in public places hoping that the child would be found, or abandoned in remote areas. John Boswell summarizes the tragic results of these foundling homes: "A minority returned to society in their teens, anonymous and stigmatized, but more fortunate than the greater numbers who died in infancy or early childhood."[19]

Another way children were raised by others was the practice of oblation, where infants or children were left at the monastery to be raised by the members of the order. Still other children were sold by their parents. More fortunate children were sent to live in foster arrangements, either where the biological parent would pay a small amount

---

16. Bainton, *Women of the Reformation*, 23.
17. Harrington, *Unwanted Child*, 9.
18. McLaughlin, "Survivors and Surrogates," 122.
19. Boswell, *Kindness of Strangers*, 432.

to the foster parent, or where the child was essentially given away to the foster parent.[20] Children occasionally lived outside the home when they were apprenticed to learn a trade, or in Martin and Katie Luther's case, when they were sent to live with relatives.

Some of the more desperate of these situations illustrate the compassionate care of the Luther's and others of their time who took in children in need from relatives and others who were not able to adequately care for them. Luther may have shown a bit of his motivation for this care in an exchange with his son Hans when Luther was very sick in July of 1527: "O you good little boy, I commend my dear Katy and you to my dear good God; you have nothing, but God, who is the Father of the orphan and the Judge of the widow, will protect you and provide for you."[21]

Luther had a theological understanding of God's care for the orphan and widow that likely informed his own care for those in need in his family, and that can also inspire us today. In this, he stands in the great Christian tradition in both East and West of caring for orphans and children in need.[22]

Fast-forward 500 years to today and there are still children in desperate need. We fortunately never hear of bodies of abandoned infants found floating in a river, but we occasionally hear of young children found dead after being left alone in an apartment that caught fire. In the United States today we have designated places like fire stations or hospitals as safe places where a parent can leave an infant for care with no questions asked. Certainly infant mortality is much lower, and our system of care for

---

20. Ibid., 206–8.
21. Smith, *Luther's Table Talk*, 407.
22. Miller, *Orphans of Byzantium*, 43–48.

children is much advanced from the Middle Ages, yet there is much to be reformed and many ways for Christians and churches to take up God's call to care for, defend, and protect the orphan and widow, just as the Luther's did.

It has been said that the foster care system of today is the equivalent of a modern-day orphanage. As of 2014, there were nearly 400,000 children across the United States in the foster care system.[23] These children in need are found sheltered in motel rooms with state social workers, or in foster or residential homes for children and youth. They are not always visible, and churches have not always recognized the need. It is easy to imagine that this sort of work is the job of the State, instead of joining with Luther in recognizing the joy of participating with God in the work of caring for the most vulnerable among us.

Fortunately, there are organizations today that exist to support congregations and Christian families in caring for children and families in need in the community. Safe Families for Children is one such organization.[24] Founded in Chicago in 2003, Safe Families works with churches to provide voluntary host homes for children of families in crisis. One of the goals of Safe Families is to prevent abuse and neglect by intervening early in a crisis. A biological parent can have a child placed with a Safe Family by contacting the local Safe Families office, provided that a suitable host family can be found.

These host families come from volunteers from churches, and are not paid. They are supported by others in their congregation with meals, transportation, babysitting, and occasionally financial help. The host families are screened similarly to foster families, with background

---

23. KIDS COUNT data Center, "Children 0 to 17 in Foster Care."
24. Safe Families for Children, "Safe Families for Children."

checks, fingerprints, and home studies to ensure that the house can be a safe home for a child. Churches can become involved with this ministry and help support children and families in their community by intervening in the midst of the crisis, before abuse or neglect occurs.

Other nonprofit agencies assist with recruiting, certifying, and supporting foster families, and helping with adoption. Some churches have specifically developed orphan care ministries, that focus on supporting and resourcing foster parents. In the Seattle area, there is a movement afoot through Seattle's Union Gospel Mission and its Light Up the City network to come alongside and support local Child and Family Services offices, social workers, and foster children.[25] These initiatives are just some of the ways that we can emulate Martin and Katie Luther's care for children and youth in need.

LUTHER'S PRACTICAL CARE FOR CHILDREN AND YOUTH

Finally, it is also helpful to consider Martin Luther's own words and actions in caring for his own children and that of others. Beginning with Philippe Aries' *Centuries of Childhood*,[26] debate has raged over the relative levels of affection that medieval parents had for their children. Aries and other scholars suggested that medieval parents cared less for their children than modern parents, likely because of high infant mortality rates and differing cultural attitudes toward children.[27] Still other scholars refuted the most extreme of these claims, and showed how medieval

25. Light up the City, "LUTC Quarterly Gathering Recap."
26. Aries, *Centuries of Childhood*.
27. Harrington, *Unwanted Child*, 2–3.

parents loved and cherished their children similar to today's parents.[28]

A look at Luther's words and actions shows the consideration and thought that he gave to the experience of youth and childhood and his own love and care for his own children. This single example does not end the debate, but it does support the claims of those scholars who would claim more continuity in parental love between medieval and modern times. Painter and Bruce both noted Luther's careful observation of children, which showed the value that he placed on them.[29] Luther theorized that human life goes through stages every seven years: infancy, childhood (beginning at age seven), starting to understand the world and be educated (age fourteen), marriage (age twenty-one), householders (age twenty-eight), magistrates in church and state (age thirty-five), and lastly kings (age forty-two).[30] After that time, Luther noticed that the senses begin to decline as the person ages.

Luther's observation of children also aided in his pedagogical recommendations. He thought of a device with two little bags with pockets in them as a way to teach children about faith and love, and remarked about this innovation: "Let no one think himself too wise, and disdain such child's play. When Christ wished to teach men, he became a man. If we are to teach children, we must become children. Would to God we had more of this child's play! We should then see in a short time a great treasure

---

28. Ibid.

29. Painter, *Luther on Education*, 154; Bruce, *Luther as an Educator*, 100–101.

30. From Luther's *Table Talks*: Bruce, *Luther as an Educator*, 100.

of Christian people, souls rich in the Scriptures and in the knowledge of God."[31]

Luther clearly valued the simple, joyous, and unhindered play of children, and recommended as well becoming like children in order to teach them. One can see this example played out in Luther's kind, gentle, and playful letter to his son Hans in 1530. In this letter, Luther describes: "a lovely, pleasant garden where many children are, they wear golden jackets and gather nice apples under the trees and pears and cherries and purple and yellow plums, and sing and run and jump and are happy and have pretty little ponies with golden reins and silver saddles."[32]

The point of this story is that the children who play in the garden are those who, "gladly pray, learn, and are good."[33] This is Luther's loving attempt as a father to get down on his son's level, and lovingly and tenderly motivate him with a story about a garden in which he would no doubt love to visit and play. It is a glimpse inside the kind, father's heart that Luther had for his children.

---

31. Painter, *Luther on Education*, 155.
32. Bruce, *Luther as an Educator*, 99.
33. Ibid.

2

Luther and Education

Like nearly everything else in comparing sixteenth-century Germany to the United States in the twenty-first century, the differences in education are difficult to comprehend. My children have grown up in largely the same highly rationalized system of modern, public education that I experienced growing up. While writing this chapter, my wife and I sent our youngest child, Tessa, off to her first day of kindergarten. In our school district, kindergarten is now a full day for all students, so each five-year-old child is guaranteed this education. Prior to her starting school, we had a conference with her teacher to talk about some of the unique attributes of Tessa that could affect her learning, as the teacher did with every other student in the class.

We are assured that Tessa's teacher, and those for our two older children, have met school district and state standards as certified teachers. Though college is not guaranteed, every U.S. student is assured a twelfth-grade education if they fulfill the minimum behavior and academic requirements. Public school students now learn from curricula approved by school boards or the state. Common and approved textbooks are used, and there is a lively public debate over best practices and standards in teaching. Having grown up in this system, and parented children in this same system, it is difficult to imagine education being otherwise. However, early sixteenth-century Germany had none of these practices widely in place to ensure the education of the young.

We don't know precisely when Luther entered school in the town of Mansfeld, but we do know that he was about seven years old, and that it was a much different experience than that of my children. In Luther's day, there was no compulsory education. Families could choose whether or not to send their children to school. Also, the State was rarely involved in education. There was little or no certification for teachers, no standardized requirements for students, and no widespread State funding of education. Parents and the students themselves often had to bear the costs of education.

Education in the Middle Ages was difficult to come by and lacking by today's standards. There were essentially three classes during much of the Middle Ages: the clergy, who were the most educated, the nobility, who were educated mainly in war and hunting, and the peasants, who were largely unschooled. "The monasteries were the repositories of knowledge and the monks, together with some of the more intelligent parish priests, were dispensers of it, meager and limited though it was."[1] For much of the Middle Ages, the ability to read and write was limited to the clergy, and most people did not see any need for it. Books were primarily written in Latin, instead of the

1. Bruce, *Luther as an Educator*, 25.

vernacular languages, and there seemed little benefit for most people to learn to read or write.[2]

As a new merchant class began to arise, however, schools were needed to train students for these endeavors. These schools taught reading, writing, and arithmetic, and they eventually evolved into city schools, where Latin was added as well.[3] The teachers for these schools largely came from the ranks of the clergy, but there were also many unskilled, itinerant men who travelled from town to town making their living as teachers in these schools.[4] Pedagogical method largely consisted of the memorization of lectures and dictated lessons, and discipline was often severe, as Luther experienced.[5]

Instead of an organized system of publicly funded elementary and secondary schools, and optional university education that is enjoyed today, there was a bewildering variety educational options in late medieval Germany. Along with the town or burgher schools, there were also monastic schools, cathedral schools, parochial schools, and knightly education. F.V.N. Painter summarizes the poor educational prospects for common people: "The ecclesiastical schools were designed chiefly for candidates for the priesthood; the parochial schools fitted the young for Church membership; the burgher schools were intended for the commercial and artisan classes of the cities; knightly education gave a training for chivalry. Thus the laboring classes were left to toil on in ignorance and want;

---

2. Ibid., 43.
3. Ibid., 44–45.
4. Painter, *Luther on Education*, 84.
5. Bruce, *Luther as an Educator*, 45.

they remained in a dependent and servile condition, their lives unillumined by intellectual pleasures."[6]

Luther's early schooling experiences were unhappy. He paints a picture of his elementary educators as, "tyrants and executioners," the schools were "prisons and hells," and "in spite of blows, trembling, fear, and misery, nothing was ever taught."[7] Luther describes being whipped fifteen times one morning for failing to repeat from memory something that he was never actually taught.[8]

However, some good did come of his time in school at Mansfeld. He learned to read and write, some simple math, and the rudiments of Latin grammar. He also had some basic Christian teaching, developed a good foundation for his use of German, as well as a love for music and singing.[9]

From Mansfeld, at thirteen years old, Luther next went to a school in Magdeberg for a year. He supported himself there by singing and begging, and was ill for a time. This school was run by the Lollards, or The Brethren of the Common Life.[10] After Magdeburg, Luther was sent to the School of St. George in Eisenach, attending it for four years.[11] He spent some time singing and begging again, until he found a benefactor who allowed him to stay in her home. At Eisenach, Luther studied Latin, history,

---

6. Painter, *Luther on Education*, 87.
7. Koestlin, *Life of Luther*, 16.
8. Ibid.
9. Bruce, *Luther as an Educator*, 59–61.
10. Ibid., 61.
11. Ibid., 62–63.

literature, and music.[12] This was a much better experience for Luther that he fondly remembered later in his life.[13]

In May of 1501, at seventeen years old, Luther matriculated at the University of Erfurt. He thrived there as a student, earning his bachelor's degree in one year, and his master's degree less than three years later.[14] Upon completing his master's degree, Luther was preparing for a career in law when he was caught in a thunderstorm and famously vowed to become a monk. He entered the Augustinian order, and devoted himself to theological studies, as well as the other requirements and activities of his order. Luther's previous academic degrees did not prepare him to teach theology, so he continued his formal academic studies at the University of Wittenberg. In 1509, he was awarded the Bachelor of Sacred Scriptures degree, and in 1512, he became a licentiate, and then Doctor of Theology.[15]

It can be easily seen from Luther's early educational experience that there were many needs to address when it came to educational reform, and this became a keen interest for Luther as well as other reformers. In 1519, just two years after posting his ninety-five theses, Luther initiated several overtures toward educational reform and better care for German children and youth in *A Sermon on the Estate of Marriage*. After speaking of marriage as a sacrament, and a covenant of fidelity, Luther turns to the subject of children: "But this at least all married people should know. They can do no better work and nothing more valuable either for God, for Christendom, for all the world, for

---

12. Ibid., 65.
13. Ibid.
14. Kittelson, *Luther the Reformer*, 13–16.
15. Koestlin, *Life of Luther*, 76–80.

themselves, and for their children than to bring up their children well."[16]

Luther felt that this third point on raising children well was even more important than the two previous on fidelity and marriage as a sacrament. He went on to say that, "There is no greater tragedy in Christendom than spoiling children. If we want to help Christendom, we most certainly have to start with the children, as happened in earlier times."[17]

For Luther, the idea of raising children well necessarily involved instructing them in the Christian faith, and he produced several works intended to help lay adults and families learn about the Christian faith. These included, "sermons on the Ten Commandments (1518), an explanation of the Lord's Prayer (1519), a 'Little Prayer Book' subtitled 'How to Pray: Instructions for Children' (1522),"[18] and the Greater and Shorter Catechisms of 1529. However, this primary emphasis on Christian instruction in the home was to undergo some changes during the turbulent decade of the 1520s.

As the Reformation progressed, funding for schools became an issue where the Roman Catholic Church was being displaced. By 1524, "Luther and his colleagues saw schools approaching a state of desolation."[19] Furthermore, "It was also becoming manifest that parents were neglecting their duty of supervising Christian upbringing in their homes. Some lacked the piety for it, others did not seem to concern themselves about their offspring's welfare, were

---

16. Luther, "A Sermon on the Estate of Marriage," 390.
17. Ibid.
18. Strauss, *Luther's House of Learning*, 4.
19. Ibid., 6.

too busy, or did not know how to do it."[20] Added to those issues were the peasant uprisings and the knights' revolt, which ultimately caused Luther to doubt the ability of the average family to effectively educate and raise their children without significant help.

Luther then, in 1524, began to advocate for public schools supported in part by the State in his *Letter to the Mayors and Aldermen of All the Cities of Germany in Behalf of Christian Schools*. Luther began by noting that his concern for the children and schools of Germany was motivated by God: "For whatever I may be in myself, I can boast with a clear conscience before God that I am not seeking my own interest, (which would be best served by silence,) but the interest of all Germany, according to the mission, (doubt it who will,) with which God has honored me."[21]

Luther believed that the right instruction of youth was not insignificant. It is "a matter in which Christ and all the world are concerned."[22] Even more poignantly, Luther asked: "And what would it avail if we possessed and performed all else, and became perfect saints, if we neglect that for which we chiefly live, namely, to care for the young? In my judgment, there is no other outward offense that in the sight of God so heavily burdens the world, and deserves such heavy chastisement, as the neglect to educate children."[23]

Luther next tabulated the reasons why parents were deficient in their obligation to raise their children well and why State officials must then take up the responsibility for helping to raise those children. He described some parents

20. Ibid.
21. Painter, *Luther on Education*, 170.
22. Ibid., 173.
23. Ibid., 178.

as being lazy, unqualified, or too busy to help educate, train, and raise their children well. City officials must then step in to educate its people to provide an informed, trained populace who can contribute to the good of the city.[24]

Luther reasoned that even if men and women did not have souls, and if schools were not needed for Christian teaching, that the best schools would still be needed because, "the maintenance of civil order and the proper regulation of the household, needs accomplished and well-trained men and women."[25] However, Luther's recommendation in 1524 is still very different from the way schools operate today. He suggested that most boys and girls should spend an hour or two per day in school, and the rest of the time either working at home or learning a trade.[26]

Luther was not at all against children playing (as was shown previously), but he knew that this would come naturally and did not need a recommendation. For the brightest pupils who showed promise for becoming teachers, preachers, or workers (presumably boys), Luther recommended that they spend more time in school to achieve their potential.[27] Finally, to close the letter, Luther made a plea for libraries to accompany schools in larger cities that could afford them.[28]

Luther thus moved from an emphasis on home instruction, to an emphasis on public school instruction for the good of the community as a whole. In 1530, Luther continued his cries for educational reform, and

24. Ibid., 180–81.
25. Ibid., 196.
26. Ibid., 199–200.
27. Ibid., 200.
28. Ibid., 203.

he advocated strongly for parents to send their children to school in his *Sermon on the Duty of Sending Children to School*. He began the sermon with some vigorous denunciations of those who would keep their children from going to school. Apparently some thought that without a future in the priesthood for their children, that there was little need of school for them.[29] This sermon was addressed to pastors, who could encourage their flocks to send their children to school to provide for the churches and the common good of society.

The first part of the sermon concerned the spiritual benefit of supporting schools, and Luther began by extolling the virtues of the clerical office, which he says included, "the duties of pastor, teacher, reader, chaplain, sexton, and school-master..."[30] He exhorted the people to remember that they need excellent ministers, and the only way to get those people is to send their children to school to potentially be trained for that office. He then reminded his listeners that, "There is no more precious treasure, no nobler thing on earth, than a pious, faithful pastor or preacher."[31]

Given the preciousness of faithful pastors, it then naturally followed for the volatile Luther that a parent who kept a child from that office was "the most impious and hurtful of men," who would depart with Satan into the abyss of hell.[32] Further, "such people are no better than Satan himself, because they are so hostile to God and the world, that they help to overthrow religion and social

---

29. Ibid., 215.
30. Ibid., 220.
31. Ibid., 224.
32. Ibid., 233.

order, and faithfully serve the devil."³³ Luther was never one to mince words when he felt that something of crucial importance was on the line.

The second part of the sermon concerned the temporal benefits of supporting schools, which, for Luther, were somewhat less than the spiritual benefits, yet were still instituted by God and thus very important. The importance of civil government, he believed, was that it protects people and property, and keeps society from degenerating into the strong dominating the weak. So Luther exhorted parents whose children could serve this way to "Think of your son as a messenger in the empire, an apostle of the emperor, a cornerstone and foundation of temporal peace on earth!"³⁴ Instead of condemning them to hell, Luther told parents that if they kept their children from those offices, that, "You must either be insensible creatures, or else you do not love your children."³⁵

Luther continued the sermon with some disturbing rhetorical questions regarding the failure of parents in sending their children to school:

> Ought not God to be angry? Ought not famine to come? Ought not pestilence, toil, the French, and other plagues, to find us out? Ought not savage tyrants to reign? Ought not war and strife to arise? Ought not bad government to prevail in the German States? Ought not Turks and Tartars to plunder us? Yea, it would be no wonder if God should open the doors and windows of hell, and let all the devils loose upon us, or if He should rain fire and brimstone from heaven and

---

33. Ibid., 234.
34. Ibid., 247.
35. Ibid., 248.

sink us all in the abyss of hell, as He did Sodom and Gomorrah.[36]

He ended the sermon by taking it a step beyond what he advocated in 1524: compulsory public education by the civil authorities.[37] It was no longer enough to ask, plead with, and threaten parents to send their children to school—the need was too great. Now Luther took the step towards mandatory public education. He reasoned that if government can compel its subjects to military service, then it should also be able to compel its subjects to education. If a child was poor, his or her education would be paid for by property of the Church, including scholarships from wealthy members of the community.[38]

So the progression of thought from Luther and the other reformers went from a preference for home instruction, to pleading with parents to send their children to school, to advocating mandatory public education. So what was the result of Luther and the other reformers' work in improving education in Germany? It was successful in at least two ways.

First, "Organizationally at least, this endeavor must be counted a success. In every German state, primary and secondary schools were built up, enlarged, equipped, ably staffed (more or less), tied together in sequence, and given fully articulated teaching programs and a clear sense of mission."[39] Because Luther and the other reformers were successful in addressing the relative chaos of late medieval popular education, an early modern system of schooling began to emerge in Protestant Germany.

36. Ibid., 266.
37. Ibid., 269.
38. Ibid., 270.
39. Strauss, "The Social Function of Schools," 195.

Second, the work of Luther and the reformers began to reach a broader spectrum of society with education. Norma Cook Everist writes, "This was a significant breakthrough. No longer was education merely for boys who might enter the priesthood. No longer was education merely for nobility. Luther goes beyond mere pity for the poor. He assumes they can learn. He cares about the rich, the poor, men, women, boys, and girls from all stations of life. He honors them by his care."[40] Luther and the other reformers believed that all of society would be benefited by greater educational opportunities. Thus, they reached out to the widest range of people, to help improve both the Church and the State.

One might wonder what motivated Luther to care about the education of children and youth in Germany. Certainly there were practical concerns that have been mentioned. Churches needed qualified pastors, schools needed educated and talented teachers, and governments needed capable leaders and administrators.

Though Luther's theological inspirations for these educational innovations are not always explicitly addressed, I believe that Luther's teachings on stations and vocations and his eschatology likely inspired his educational reform efforts. Even if not explicitly inspiring them, these beliefs at least are congruent with what Luther was seeking to accomplish.

Luther taught that there are many various stations in life that God uses to preserve humanity, and establish order, justice, and peace in the world.[41] These stations can be organized under three categories: marriage and family (which included business and the economy), ministry

---

40. Everist, "Luther on Education," 80.
41. Althaus, *Ethics of Martin Luther*, 37.

Luther and Education

(including clergy and related religious professions), and secular authority (including princes, judges, civil officers, and others).[42] These stations were divinely instituted, each necessary to complement the others, and each worthy of equal respect and honor.[43]

The connection with education necessarily follows from this understanding in a practical way. Society could not flourish, and these divinely instituted stations could not function without educated clergy, business leaders, and government officials to fulfill their vocations. Norma Cook Everist summarizes the connection this way:

> Luther's emphasis on the priesthood of all believers creates a connection between religion and daily life. The freedom Christian people experience thrusts them forth into the world in their vocation. Yet how can people fulfill those vocations without education? No one can be left in ignorance, no matter what their class. Education becomes the interest of the state no less than that of the church. Its aim should be to fit the young for useful living in every relation.[44]

So, without proper educational opportunities, the prospects of anyone adequately performing in their God-given stations are considerably diminished.

In addition to Luther's understanding of vocation, his eschatology also complemented his emphasis on education. Gerhard Forde talks about just how puzzling it was for some when Luther married in 1525.[45] Luther, as well as many of his contemporaries, eagerly expected

42. Ibid., 36–37.
43. Ibid., 37.
44. Everist, "Luther on Education," 78–79.
45. Forde, *Where God Meets Man*, 95–98.

and anticipated the coming Day of the Lord, which would bring decisive and irreversible changes to the world. The question then, as it could be today, is about what a person would do if they knew the world would end the next day. Would it be best to pray and be especially penitent, or to experience something novel before everything changes, or perhaps to have one last drunken party before it all ends?

In marrying, Luther chose a far different option. "The nearness of the end made it imperative to become a true *creature* of God, a human being."[46] Luther's desire to get married was about embracing his true nature as a created being, instead of mistakenly attempting to escape this earth through pious actions. "So because of the nearness of the end, because of his faith in the world 'to come,' Luther is persuaded not to leave this world, not to despise it, but to enter into it all the more fully and take up its concerns and tasks all the more seriously."[47]

Luther did not choose to act more "spiritual," or even to overindulge his fleshly desires, but instead chose to embrace more fully his role in the world. Forde explains that Luther's eschatology lay behind Luther's belief, "that everyone should enter into his worldly vocation in the confidence that it is pleasing to God, and look on it as a commission from God."[48] So it made sense that Luther would be passionately concerned about the education of children and youth in his time. The anticipation of the end should motivate each person to fully embrace their vocation, and the only way that could fully be possible is for the best educational opportunities to be available to the widest range of people.

46. Ibid., 96.
47. Ibid., 97.
48. Ibid., 98.

Luther and Education

As previously explained, the differences are great between public education in the twenty-first century United States and the sixteenth century German states. In Luther's day, Christian and public secular education easily and naturally mixed together in schools, where today that is not the case. However, it is clear that Luther believed that both forms of learning were crucial to the functioning of a healthy church and society. So, whereas Luther's work on faith formation for children and youth will be covered in the following chapter, the remainder of this chapter will focus on what Luther's advocacy for public, secular education could mean for us today.

Public schools are a crucial part of every community. When they are thriving, they can be an important place of learning and connection for members of the community. But when they are struggling, they often exemplify the difficult challenges of the community of which they are a part. Churches can play a unique role in helping to support public schools, and fortunately partnerships like this are on the rise. Today, many churches are taking up Luther and the reformers' charge to support schools in their mission to educate children and youth.

There are several ways that churches today can and have supported schools in fulfilling their educational mission with children and youth. The most obvious way is to support schools with educational initiatives such as tutoring or academic help. But this just begins to scratch the surface of ways that churches can support and partner with schools. There are a wide range of needs that can be addressed, from volunteering and facility maintenance, to after-school activities, or material support for children and families in need.

Peace Lutheran Church in the Hilltop neighborhood of Tacoma, Washington, is one such congregation that has taken significant steps in partnering with local schools to address some substantial educational needs in their neighborhood.[49] It began with a process of listening, where the pastor would visit the people in his surrounding neighborhood, just to pray and hear what the needs were. From this process of listening and discernment, the congregation gained a vision for educational support for the many struggling elementary, middle, and high school students around them.

This culminated in spinning off a separate nonprofit organization to address the educational needs: Peace Community Center. Over the years, the work of Peace Community Center has grown, so that in 2015 it had programs to assist elementary through college students. Its staff and budget have grown with the expanded programs, so that it now far exceeds the church that originally birthed the nonprofit.

This is an extraordinary example of a neighborhood experiencing dire needs, where the Spirit birthed an amazing vision and a nonprofit organization to meet those needs. This example may go beyond what is possible for most churches, and the many churches and individuals who are providing tutoring and academic support on a much smaller level should be equally valued and celebrated.

It is difficult, or nearly impossible, to separate academic help from the many other needs that are a part of a child's life. Peace Community Center recognizes this through its many programs, as well as many other churches who provide assistance to children and youth in their

---

49. The following story came from an interview with the executive director of Peace Community Center in 2012.

Luther and Education

communities. Another example is the "On the Corner" program from Central Lutheran Church in Yakima, Washington. This program focuses on developing social, physical, emotional, and academic skills by using a variety of different options for students, including homework assistance, music, reading, a computer lab, games, and service projects.[50]

Some churches focus instead on a partnership with a local school. SouthLake Church in West Linn, Oregon, is an extraordinary example of this kind of partnership. In 2008, SouthLake Church began serving at Roosevelt High School in a particularly challenging part of Portland, Oregon, about twenty-five miles from SouthLake's location.[51] SouthLake began with a simple desire to serve the school by organizing a "Day of Service," that offered assistance with landscaping, painting, and cleaning projects at the school. Fortunately, the desire to serve Roosevelt High School did not end there, and SouthLake became passionate about continuing this work after seeing the success of this first endeavor. SouthLake's members began to help with coaching, they opened a clothing bank, and they attended school athletic activities to support the students. The partnership has gone so far as to have a "site coordinator" from the church with an office at the school, to better know the needs of the school, and to be able to coordinate the volunteers from the church and community.

Stories like this one from SouthLake have birthed citywide, regional, and even national initiatives to connect public schools with church partners. Inspired by SouthLake's work, the Luis Palau Association (based in

50. Central Lutheran Church, "Welcome to On the Corner!"

51. The story of SouthLake's partnership with Roosevelt High School is told in the DVD documentary: Martin, *Undivided*.

Portland, Oregon) caught the vision for church-school partnerships as well. In March of 2012, in partnership with Portland Public Schools, the School Partnership Network was born with the goal of finding partners like SouthLake for each of the over 400 public schools in the greater Portland/Vancouver metropolitan area.[52] By 2013, there were documented church partners for 250 of the 471 public schools in the region, which is an astounding accomplishment.[53]

In other parts of the country, similar initiatives to link churches with public schools are also taking place. Loving Houston is an initiative to support partnerships between churches and schools similar to those in the Portland area. In Dallas, Texas, The Turn-Around Agenda (a ministry of Oak Cliff Bible Fellowship) works with sixty-one public schools in the county through its Public Schools Outreach program.[54] This program is being promoted as a national model through the National Church Adopt-a-School Initiative.[55] SouthLake Church also has dreams for school and church partnerships to catch fire nationally, and it is promoting that effort through a documentary DVD and their website.[56]

There are many, many other exciting stories of churches and individuals who have in small and big ways begun to get involved with what God is doing in creating a future for this world through the education of children and youth. Some utilize drop-in after school programs, while

52. CityServe Portland, "History."
53. CityServe Portland, "School Partnership Network Reaches Significant Milestone."
54. The Turn Around Agenda, "Public Schools Outreach (PSO)."
55. "National Church Adopt-A-School Initiative."
56. "Be|Undivided."

Luther and Education

others create close partnerships with local schools. Some host breakfasts, or art therapy classes, or help with providing school supplies for children in need.

In Louisville, Kentucky, there is even an initiative among schools and churches to integrate national Common Core standards into VBS curricula to combat the "summer slide," where students tend to regress academically over the summer.[57] There are no limits to the ways that churches can be involved with supporting education, only the key requirement to listen carefully to the needs of the surrounding community and to discern the Spirit's leading.

Of course, much could be said about the ways that individuals could be involved on their own as well, as coaches, teachers, PTA volunteers, mentors, tutors, and more. Further, Luther's response to the need for educational reform should not limit churches and individuals from recognizing God's leading to be involved in other aspects of the lives of children and youth in their communities as well. No doubt, in listening to neighbors, community members and leaders, there are many more areas that can be addressed in order for children and youth to thrive.

I believe that this type of work with youth in the community is the beginning of a truly missional youth ministry, which does not view community youth simply as objects to be added to church membership rolls, but instead as beloved creations of God in and of themselves. As such, these youth are deserving of our love, care, and respect with no hidden agenda, as we recognize, as Luther did, that providing the basis for excellent educational opportunities is part of God's mission in the world. We have an amazing opportunity and gift in this time to be able to

---

57. Lee, "Common Core Meets VBS."

participate in God's mission, and to be a significant part of the lives of children and youth in our communities. Let us join in this endeavor as we follow the Spirit's leading.

3

Luther and Faith Formation

It seems a nearly universal human assumption that there is something more pristine and pure about the past. Times were simpler, people were more moral, and life, though still flawed, was less complex and easier to navigate. Billionaire celebrity Donald Trump made a lot of waves in the 2016 Presidential race with his slogan, "Make America Great Again." The saying hearkens back to a time of clear moral choices, when America stood astride the world in power, greatness, and uncompromising moral certitude.

Of course this America never really existed, just as our other fantasies of pristine pasts never existed either. I think this is true for Christian catechesis as well. Martin Luther began by imagining faith formation primarily taking place in the home. One could imagine the faithful German families of the 1500s gathering little Hans and Greta by the fireside as they eagerly awaited instruction in the Christian faith from their involved, caring, and educated parents.

While there may have been a handful of families who lived out this ideal, it is far from the reality that confronted Luther and his fellow reformers. From 1526 to 1530, Luther and other reformers visited churches in Saxony to address issues with the income and education of pastors, and assess the state of the Reformation among the people.[1] They found rough, crude people who enjoyed too much beer and sex and who didn't care much for Christian doctrine or worship services.[2] It sounds like essentially the equivalent of a modern college fraternity house.

The question, then, for the reformers, was how to address the widespread intemperate living and ignorance of Christian doctrine amongst a people for whom they cared deeply. This was not to mention the lack of theological education among pastors and the crucial need for parents to gain the interest and ability to effectively educate their children in the basics of Christian beliefs. As a solution to these ills, and in response to the many competing versions of Christian beliefs among the Anabaptists, Catholics, Zwinglians, and others, Luther composed his Small and Large catechisms.

The Small Catechism was meant originally as a book for the family—a handbook for Christian belief and living. Fathers were urged to teach it to their household, as that was their responsibility and duty in the era's patriarchal society. However, the reformers also knew that this was not enough. Nicolaus von Amsdorf and Christoph Fischer, both contemporaries of Luther and his fellow reformers, gave their sad summaries on the state of Christian instruction in the home less than twenty years after Luther's death:

---

1. Arand, *That I May Be His Own*, 72.
2. My summary of ibid, 73.

> Writing in his seventy-eighth year, the naturally pessimistic Amsdorf said flatly that he was moved to compose his admonition on parental review of the sermon because there was not a father left in Germany who was carrying out his God-given responsibility of instructing his children. Fischer shared Amsdorf's concern. Many parents were raising their children not for the Lord but for the devil, he lamented at the conclusion of a passage in which he had stressed the catechism as one means by which children are raised for the Lord.[3]

Given that parents could not be completely trusted with the religious instruction of their families, the Small Catechism was also taught through sermons and examinations in churches, and it was used in schools as a textbook for learning.

The catechism is a rich and deep subject, and many directions could be explored here. However, this chapter will focus on the relevance of the Small Catechism for the faith formation of children and youth, and what it could mean for us today. In order to do this, it is important to understand the context in which faith formation occurs, both in Luther's time and today. After looking at the difficult environment that confronted Luther, and the use of catechisms in Christian history, this chapter will next address the particularities of our own context. Finally, some suggestions will be made as to what Luther's contributions to faith formation and specifically his catechisms could mean for children's and youth workers today.

---

3. Kolb, "The Layman's Bible," 22.

CATECHISMS IN CHRISTIAN HISTORY

The use of a catechism in Christian faith formation was not pioneered by Luther. In fact, it was a common practice throughout much of church history. Traditionally, Christians considered the Creed, the Lord's Prayer, and some sort of moral teaching like the Ten Commandments as crucial elements of Christian teaching that every Christian should know.[4] These three elements were the core of Christian catechisms, to which other materials were often added as well.[5]

The innovations that made Luther's catechism especially relevant to his day were his linking of it to evangelical doctrine and its simple form allowing easy memorization by often largely illiterate children and adults. This powerful combination served to further the cause of the reformation as his catechism was adopted and adapted for instructing the young in schools, homes, and churches, and was preached regularly in Protestant regions across Germany throughout the church year. Its widespread translation and continued use over the past 500 years is a testament to its clarity, simplicity, and power to help form Christian faith among young and old alike.

Luther's Small Catechism took elements of catechisms common to the Christian tradition, but he uniquely rearranged them and added additional pieces to craft his own unique contribution to Christian faith formation. Charles Arand argues that a catechism should not be thought of primarily as a book of questions and answers, as much as it should be identified specifically with anything including the Ten Commandments, the Apostles' Creed, and

---

4. Arand, *That I May Be His Own*, 29.
5. Ibid., 41.

Luther and Faith Formation

the Lord's Prayer.[6] Luther took these three pieces of biblical and confessional literature, and combined them with sections on Baptism, the Lord's Supper, confession, daily prayers, a Table of Christian Callings, and marriage and baptismal services.[7]

Luther arranged the Small Catechism according to his evangelical principles, with the Decalogue first (to show the need for God through the Law), the Creed second (to show what to believe), and the Lord's Prayer third (to show how to pray). The sacraments followed as tangible ways to experience the grace of God.

For many today, a catechism can seem dated and foreign. Non-Lutheran Christian churches across the United States see little use for any catechism, let along Luther's catechisms. Though literacy in the United States is far more common than in Reformation Germany, many similar problems remain today that resemble those that Luther and the other reformers faced.

I have yet, in all the churches I have attended or worked, to find a congregation where many parents are actively instructing their children in the faith at home. Perhaps I have just not attended the right churches. But it seems more likely that problems today are similar to Luther's time, and parents do not have the time, ability or interest to effectively educate and form their children in the basics of Christian belief and practice. I know that my home is not much different than others in the churches I have worked in and attended either.

With the separation of Church and State in the United States, public schools will, of course, not be forming children in Christian faith either. So this essentially leaves

6. Ibid., 22.
7. Ibid., 41–47.

pastors, children's and youth workers with the difficult task of taking on much of the challenge of forming the faith of the young. One can lament this fact, but it remains, and children's and youth workers need to effectively work in this environment. So just as Luther faced a frat house environment, what is the cultural context that faces children's and youth workers today as they attempt the challenging work of attending to the faith formation of the young? I believe several aspects of the current context are important to highlight: Moralistic Therapeutic Deism, increasing ethnic diversity and affiliational options for youth, and the rise of user-generated content.

CURRENT CULTURAL CONTEXT

Moralistic Therapeutic Deism

Though now over ten years old, the National Study of Youth and Religion remains one of the most thorough and comprehensive research studies on teen spirituality and religious belief.[8] After sifting through and analyzing the survey and interview data, the researchers proposed a tentative hypothesis that the majority of teens in the United States practice a faith that has colonized traditional religions without respect for denominational boundaries. Though this faith may bear some similarities to each religious tradition, it is markedly different from each one and does not resemble the traditional teachings of the Christian faith within the United States. The researchers

---

8. It included 3,370 telephone surveys and 267 in-depth interviews with youth between thirteen and seventeen years old in forty-five different states. Smith and Denton, *Soul Searching*, 292, 302.

Luther and Faith Formation

labeled this colonizing force: "Moralistic Therapeutic Deism" (MTD).[9]

The problem with MTD for Christianity is that it closely mimics traditional versions of the faith, but it leaves out crucial pieces that are important for its functioning as a whole. The moralistic part of MTD places an importance on being good, nice, responsible, pleasant, and getting along with people. Most people would likely agree that these are better character traits than being unpleasant, rude, disrespectful, lazy, and incorrigible.

However, Christianity is about far more than "fulfilling one's personal potential, and not being socially disruptive or interpersonally obnoxious."[10] Sometimes Christians are called to take difficult stands on issues that are important to them. Sojourners CEO Jim Wallis has been arrested twenty-two times for peaceful demonstrations on issues that mattered deeply to him because of his faith.[11] Consider Jesus' radical actions in the temple to drive out the money-changers.[12] In a world filled with injustice and persecution, being nice is not enough.

The therapeutic aspect of MTD has an individualistic emphasis that places an importance on, "feeling good, happy, secure, at peace."[13] Again, it is hard to argue that these are bad qualities to possess. Yet, this stands in stark contrast to Jesus' call to take up the cross and follow him.

The way of Jesus and the cross is one of suffering, temptation, and trial. It is about being involved in the

---

9. Ibid., 162–71.

10. Ibid., 163.

11. Gilgoff, "Evangelical Minister Jim Wallis Is in Demand in Obama's Washington."

12. Matthew 21:12–13.

13. Smith and Denton, *Soul Searching*, 164.

messiest and dirtiest parts of life, facing the reality that we are all at once both saint and sinner, and coming to grips with who we really are as people. Solidarity and identification with those who are suffering most often does not lead to feeling good, happy and secure. It can be profoundly unsettling to not only face the ravaging effects of sin in the lives of others, but also to see it in one's own life. This therapeutic part of MTD flies in the face of the cross and the way of Jesus in the world.

The final part of MTD, deism, involves the knowledge that a god exists who is watching over the world. However, this god is not very personal, nor is this god trinitarian. This god is profoundly distant and mostly uninvolved with the world, except during the rare times when the MTD practitioners may call on that god to restore a sense of personal well-being. In contrast, the God of the Christian scriptures is known through Father, Son, and Holy Spirit. This God is active in the world, creating, healing, reconciling, and has called a people to participate in that work.

"Tribes" and Ethnic Diversity

Accompanying the rise of MTD, the United States is a much more diverse place then when I graduated from high school in 1991, and this new reality plays a role in faith formation as well. I grew up in the same home for my entire childhood in a suburb just north of Seattle, Washington. In my high school, I recall various discernible groups of students: popular kids, jocks, stoners, goths, a few gang members, and then the vast expanse of "the rest of us." "The rest of us" were not popular, not outcast socially, not particularly good at sports, and not into the heavy metal music of the time — just plain old mostly white kids from

Luther and Faith Formation

the suburbs. The 1990 census in my small suburb found that nearly 90 percent of the population was White, with the remainder consisting of mostly Asians and Pacific Islanders, along with small percentages of Blacks, Hispanics, American Indian and Alaska Natives.[14]

But how times have changed. The 2010 census for that same suburb found that the overall White population had decreased by 3,000 people, while the total population for the town increased by 7,000 people.[15] Whites now comprise just 64 percent of the total population, with Asian and Pacific Islanders next at 18 percent, and significant and growing Black and Hispanic populations.

The suburb where I currently live has also seen dramatic changes in that same twenty years: the percentage of Whites to the total population shrank from 83 percent to 55 percent, while the Asian and Pacific Islander population grew sixfold, the Black population tripled, and the percentage identifying as Hispanic grew almost tenfold.[16] The students in the high schools nearby report a greater diversity of potential affiliations, including divisions among racial/ethnic lines. Gone are the stoners and goths, but now a student could hang out with the geeks/gamers, Hispanics, Blacks, Asians, ravers, Otakus, preppy kids, or still be a popular kid, gang member, or a part of any number of other niche groups.

Seth Godin describes some of the changes in affiliation that have taken place in the past twenty years in his

---

14. The 1990 census data used here came from the 1990 Official (Unadjusted) and Adjusted Census Data, which can be found here: http://www.census.gov/main/www/cen1990.html.

15. The 2010 census data came from the Profile of General Population and Housing Characteristics: 2010, which can be found here: http://factfinder2.census.gov/faces/nav/jsf/pages/index.xhtml.

16. Ibid.

book, *Tribes*.[17] Whereas tribal identification has always been a part of human culture, the internet now has eliminated issues regarding geography and it is easier to connect with fellow tribe members than ever before. Moreover, there is a multiplicity of options for tribes: "smaller tribes, influential tribes, horizontal and vertical tribes, and tribes that could never have existed before. Tribes you work with, tribes you travel with, tribes you buy with. Tribes that vote, that discuss, that fight."[18]

Leading and connecting these tribes is made easier than ever before through social networking sites and technology. No doubt this diversification of options has made it easier for youth to find their place in several different niches at once, and affiliate with certain groups at their own school as well as with other non-geographical tribes. It seems likely that many other locations around the United States are experiencing similar radical changes in ethnic diversity and increasing tribal affiliational options, with all of the accompanying implications for youth ministry in a dramatically changed context.

User-generated Content

Accompanying increasing ethnic diversity and an expanding range of affiliational choices has been what Thomas Friedman has described as the flattening of the world that has taken place in the past twenty years.[19] For the purposes of this chapter, this "flattening" essentially describes a world where individuals have greater access to information, the ability to create their own information, and where

17. Seth Godin, *Tribes*, 4–5.
18. Ibid., 4.
19. Friedman, *The World Is Flat*.

communication is faster and more direct than ever, thus empowering individuals to do things they could not do before.

The flattening forces that Friedman describes include the fall of the Berlin wall in 1989, which effectively meant the end of Europe's centrally-planned communist economies and the triumph of global consumer capitalism. Students today have grown up in this entrepreneurial world, in which they must compete in a global economy. Another flattening force has been the growth of the World Wide Web and its associated technologies. This well-documented change has forever changed communication, commerce, research, and many other human endeavors.

Friedman also mentions uploading as a flattening force. Included in this idea are the rise of community-developed software programs, distributed freely on the internet, and other forms of user-generated content, like posting videos to YouTube. Students today no doubt expect to be part of the planning and execution of youth ministry, just as they have greater access to create content in other parts of their lives.

First published in 2005, Friedman's ideas about a flat world are now essentially old news. This is the sea in which we all swim. His initial observations have continued apace with the exponential rise of social networks. A 2015 report from the Pew Research Center noted that 73% of all online men used social networking sites, along with 80% of all online women.[20] The flattening of the world continues. What is important for youth ministry faith formation is to step back and note the incredible changes that have taken place in the past twenty years. The world is truly a different place

---

20. Anderson, "Men Catch up with Women on Overall Social Media Use."

for students today, and no doubt this will be worked out in the ways that students approach their youth ministries and associated ideas about faith formation.

YOUTH MINISTRY STRUCTURE

The sixteenth century world of Martin Luther would be a strange and foreign place for the youth of today, as would the world of my youth. The world for many students today is more open, diverse, flat, and participatory. This is the context in which faith formation takes place today. So, what kind of structure can best facilitate faith formation in this changed context? It is a structure that must accommodate these realities of a changed context. These realities demand a structure that allows for greater options for involvement and that is open and invites participation, where hierarchy is flattened and students are empowered to make a difference in their congregations and communities.

The type of structure that emphasizes openness, involvement, participation, and empowerment is not simply a good idea because of contextual and cultural changes. In fact, research from the Exemplary Youth Ministry study has shown that congregations with high percentages of committed Christian youth invite participation from students, parents, staff, pastors, and volunteers in significant aspects of ministry decision-making.[21]

One structure that worked well at a previous church where I worked emphasized giving students multiple ways to connect to the life of the church, instead of just emphasizing youth group, Sunday School, or confirmation attendance. We emphasized providing a diverse menu of

---

21. Martinson et al., *The Spirit and Culture of Youth Ministry*, 205–16.

options for students and families, including: before and after school programs, Sunday School classes, service activities, youth group, fun overnight events, confirmation classes, retreats, and mission trip experiences. Though this slate of options differs little from what is offered at many churches, our emphasis was on providing a way for each individual student to be able to connect with the life of the church, without expecting or worrying about whether the student made it to a weekly youth group activity.

We also emphasized that among the choices in this slate of activities for students, it was also just fine for a student to opt out altogether, and just serve, worship, and connect with the wider activities of the church outside the special youth group activities. In today's culture, not every student will be happy with preselected programmatic slots in which they must fit. We found that expecting faith formation to solely be a product of the programmatic aspects of the organized youth ministry activities was a recipe for frustration. God will show up however God wants to, despite our attempts to cajole and coerce faith from our students.

Explaining this particular structure is not an attempt to propose a one-size-fits-all solution for every church. There are as many ways to successfully do youth ministry as there are churches doing youth ministry. Others will no doubt find great success with small groups, or mentorship programs, or large and exciting youth worship services. But all of these programmatic and structural initiatives will need to address in their own way the rise of niche groups, increasing ethnic diversity, and the opportunities for students themselves to create content and shape the ministry.

INSIGHTS FROM LUTHER FOR TODAY

So what can be gleaned from Luther's Catechisms for today, given this context of diversity, choice, and the demand for flattened hierarchies and increased participation? I believe that there are several ways that Luther's pioneering attention to his context could relate to our need to address our context.

Re-engaging Parents

First, just as Luther aimed for parents to play a primary role in faith formation, so should we as well. My time learning youth ministry was probably similar to many other youth workers who began about twenty years ago. I was taught, either implicitly or explicitly, that the best way to do youth ministry was to separate the youth from their parents. Form a team of youthful college students, single adults, and parents with young children or none at all, and use them as mentors and adult Christian role models for the students. This could happen through small groups, or a youth group meeting, or youth-focused worship services. It didn't matter. The way to do youth ministry was to get these valuable volunteers to help put on youth events, teach Sunday School, lead small groups, and connect individually with youth.

Parents were essentially an afterthought in this style of ministry. I led parent meetings once or twice a year, where usually I ended up with my head in my hands afterwards, just glad that I made it through. This was, of course, a poor way to conceptualize ministry with youth, but it has had enough good results coming out of it over the years to keep sustaining it in many churches. It is certainly a good

Luther and Faith Formation

and necessary thing to connect youth with caring Christian adults, but the problem has been in diminishing and denying the crucial place of parents in the faith formation of their own children.

This model of ministry fits well with the desires of youth. At a time when they are trying on new identities and breaking away from their parents, separation fits well with where they are at. No one wants their parents around when they are trying to get to know or impress that girl or guy that they are interested in. Or even around when they are hanging out with their friends. It makes sense. But parents cannot be considered an afterthought and must be given a crucial place in the faith formation of their own children for youth and children's ministry to be effective.

Kenda Creasy Dean makes it clear: "Research is nearly unanimous on this point: parents matter most in shaping the religious lives of their children."[22] Not well intentioned youth workers or pastors, not cool young adults who are barely older than the teens themselves, but plain-old, boring, out-of-touch parents. The ones who actually have raised and loved their children since birth. Who would have thought?

After realizing this fact, and repenting of my many years of seeing parents as impediments to ministry instead of crucial partners, I began with the pastors of the church where I had been working to try to change the mindset of how we approached parents as a part of youth ministry. Fortunately, we didn't throw out all of our dedicated and important adult volunteers. Instead, we began to try to change our mindset and dream of ways that we could effectively engage parents in faith formation.

---

22. Dean, *Almost Christian*, 111.

For us, that meant addressing our confirmation program, which was one of our most crucial ways for engaging youth in faith formation, and an easy way to begin to re-involve our parents and families in youth ministry. Many parents for years had viewed confirmation exclusively as a one-year drop-off program for their youth where they would get their shot in the arm of faith, graduate at the end of the year, and essentially not look back.

We sought to change that mindset by requiring parental participation in classes that ran at the same time as the student classes. We wanted to "up the ante," so to speak, so parents understood that confirmation was not just something for their children, but it was something for them as well. This was, admittedly, a small step. And I don't know that it radically impacted the long term faith formation of our students. But it was a necessary first step that could be built upon.

Another change that was made was seeking opportunities to involve parents alongside their youth in youth ministry activities. This was not easy, as students sometimes just need a place to be away from their parents, which is a healthy and natural part of growing up, and something that needs to be accounted for in youth ministry. A natural tension exists between involving students in the life of the church with their parents, and providing space for them to explore faith more in the context of their peer group and with other caring adults.

Two places where we found parents fitting well in youth ministry were in family service projects and as Sunday School discussion leaders. It wasn't always easy, but often the youth would be able to welcome parents in Sunday School. One of my other great joys while working at this church was seeing youth serving with their families at an emergency family shelter in a nearby city. It was rewarding seeing parents connect with youth from outside their own family, and seeing everyone serve together and love families who were in need in the community.

Of course, these are far from the only ways to involve parents in youth ministry. There are as many ways to involve parents as there are churches who are willing to experiment. Some churches emphasize webs of connection that include extended family members, while others focus on providing faith formation materials for families to use at home, before bedtime or at the dinner table. Regardless of how it happens, the most important aspect is that parents are included and valued as the most important part of how their children grow in their understanding and practice of their faith.

The Small Catechism Today

Lutherans today are faced with questions about the necessity of Luther's Small Catechism in forming faith. Charles Arand and Timothy Wengert both lament the relative neglect and lack of understanding around Luther's catechisms in contemporary Lutheran churches.[23] In fact, the Small Catechism was written to be relevant in a much different time. The consensus best pedagogical method in largely illiterate sixteenth century Europe was rote questions and answers from teacher to student that aided memorization. Today, in our world of screens of many sizes, this approach would find few who would favor it. Educational theory has progressed since Luther's time.

---

23. Wengert, *Martin Luther's Catechisms*, 1; Arand, *That I May Be His Own*, 16.

It is beneficial to remember Arand's injunction that the catechism should not be considered simply by its form, but instead should be understood as anything that references the content of Decalogue, Creed, and Lord's Prayer. This opens up many options for Lutherans to connect with children and adults around these three areas, as well as the other parts of the Small Catechism. Concordia Publishing House (among others) has even published a free smartphone app that contains the 1986 translation of the Small Catechism. Boundless options exist as well to use this content in a way that is relevant for contemporary children and adults.

Another question to consider for those who are not Lutheran is the relevance of the Small Catechism for their faith tradition. While the Decalogue, Creed, and Lord's Prayer could translate well among other Christian traditions, Luther's view of the sacraments likely not would be as well received. But the question remains for all to consider: what catechetical literature are we using to form the faith of the young, or new Christians? And we all should be asking, 1) "what are the basics that are needed for Christians to know, believe, and practice?" and, 2) "how do we best communicate and model those things for our children and youth?"

These questions have not been agreed upon throughout Christian history, and they do not have easy answers. We have been given the scriptures, and we have our traditions and Christian communities, but what is most important to draw out from the scriptures? God didn't supply us with a catechism or creed. We (the church) created them as shorthand aids for learning and growth.

Today, large megachurches are especially faced with the issue of how to educate and inform masses of people on their views of the basics of Christian faith. For them, this is often accomplished through the use of a series of classes that lead people through a membership process. This is similar to the function of Luther's Small Catechism, but it has far less power as a devotional tool. Devotional books are also popular sellers in Christian bookstores, but they lack the simplicity and theological rigor of the Small Catechism. It seems that there is little today that can correspond to or compete with Luther's little work.

I submit that the best practice for Lutheran churches, and perhaps for others as well, would be to make greater use of Luther's Small Catechism. In a time where Christians desperately need to know the basics of their faith, the Small Catechism could be the answer that everyone is waiting for, but has been right under our noses.

4

Luther and Reason

In May 2015, the Pew Research Center released a report detailing America's changing religious affiliations, which was based on the 2014 U.S. Religious Landscape Study.[1] Though at the time it was the subject of great consternation among Christian leaders and bloggers, I think few people were surprised at all by what was said. The report detailed sharp losses among Catholics and mainline Protestants between 2007 and 2014. Evangelical Protestants were not immune, and suffered a slight decline as well. The group that is growing at the expense of the others is the unaffiliated, which includes atheists, agnostics, and "nothing in particular."

Many of those who work among youth in the United States have realized for some time that something is going on. Faith formation with youth has never been simple, and it has never looked like a straight line or simple equation, but it seems to be more complex now than ever before.

1. "America's Changing Religious Landscape."

Luther and Reason

Students are grappling with difficult questions and have unprecedented access to information like never before.

I often posed a question to begin a high school Sunday school class, giving everyone in the room a chance to talk. One week, I asked, "we all know that you are committed Christians, but if you could join some other religion, which one would it be?" Several answers included religions that some of their friends adhered to, or different denominations of Christianity, but one eighth-grade student proclaimed that he would follow the Flying Spaghetti Monster. That brought a collective chuckle from the class. I had heard of this internet phenomenon before, and to my surprise, so had every single student in the class.

I found few committed atheists in my middle school or high school in the late 1980s and early 1990s. But today, encountering an atheist and reading or listening to what they think of Christianity is as simple as a search on Google or YouTube. As a young Christian, I had many trusted gatekeepers who would happily answer any questions I had about my faith. I could approach my parents, pastor, youth pastor, or a teacher or adult friend for answers to difficult questions. But today, these gatekeepers can easily be circumvented if a child or youth is searching for answers to questions and is looking for a quicker solution, or simply does not want to talk to any of those trusted adults.

Many difficult questions face youths today, and many churches seem ill-equipped to answer them. When presented with evolutionary science, the first chapters of Genesis can quickly seem to be quaint ramblings of backwards tribespeople. If a youth has a friend or relative who has come out as gay, the once common Christian posture of viewing homosexuality as sinful can seem hateful at worst, or ignorant at best. Which is to say nothing of other difficult questions for Christians surrounding issues like transgendered, intersexed, or bisexual people.

In talking with friends, or in forays around the internet, a student may encounter a faith or belief system that may seem to make more sense to them than does Christianity, or at least seem equally plausible. What is a youth to do with this information? Whereas their Christian faith once seemed unassailable, it now seems to be just one option among many other possible choices. What makes Christianity special or better than any other belief system or just not believing in any deity at all?

It may not be the case in other parts of the country, but in the Pacific Northwest, where I live, the surrounding culture does not reinforce at all belief in God, or the importance of gathering weekly with other believers for worship. Seattle, along with San Francisco and Boston, are the metro areas in the nation with the lowest percentage of weekly worship attendance.[2] When you live in the great Northwest, it's much easier to participate in other activities or just stay home. And after you stay home from church a few weeks, it can make you wonder why you'd really want to go all that much anyway.

We face this and more when it comes to youth and the gospel. In a context where the unaffiliated are growing and some think the U.S. will end up like Scandinavia and Europe, what does it mean to present a gospel that makes sense in this culture? How can the gospel make sense to students today when Christianity is simply one option among many? When going to church is not really all that meaningful, and most people don't? When Christians seem hateful and ill-informed on important scientific and

---

2. "Attendance at Religious Services by Metro Area."

Luther and Reason

contemporary sexual issues? And when some options really seem to make more sense than Christianity anyway?

One response to all of these issues could be to emphasize the need for personal conversion and piety. Some argue that if a person has a genuine conversion experience, and then continues after that experience with regular prayer, bible study, and church attendance, that those practices will help guard the person from the difficult influences detailed above. Though I believe it is crucial for each person to seek guidance from God, and to nurture and tend to their faith, I don't believe that these practices alone are enough to counter the questions that are gnawing away at the edges of Christianity.

Something else is needed as well: a more robust understanding of the Christian faith that can account for the age old challenges of scientific questions, religious pluralism, biblical interpretation, and what it means to be a Christian community. A simple study of Luther's thought will not yield answers that silence all doubts. Yet, I believe that Luther's theology holds some key postures that better address our issues today, particularly regarding faith, doubt, and the place of reason in the Christian faith.

LUTHER'S INTELLECTUAL CONTEXT

It can be easy to assume that our intellectual context is vastly different than that of the sixteenth century. And in many ways, it is. However, Martin Luther's context was in some ways actually not far removed from our own. The people of Luther's day lived before the day when a triumphant scientism could confidently elbow aside religion as merely a product of an earlier time, something that could now be cast away. However, the thought of Luther's day was steeped in a rationalism of its own.

Late medieval scholastic theologians had constructed a synthesis of reason and theology that left little room for faith. Faith was simply the final small step in a process in which the way was prepared through copious rational theological arguments.[3] Luther despised the common reliance on Aristotle that characterized the theology of the day, as was initiated by Thomas Aquinas centuries earlier.[4] He doubted whether Aquinas was truly a Christian, and counseled that "a young man should flee philosophy and scholastic theology as the death of his soul."[5] "The God who is known to reason on rational grounds Luther calls a philosophical, Aristotelian God, and he says of this God, 'He means nothing to us.'"[6]

And so, against this pervasive environment where it was assumed that the things of faith could be attained through processes of reason, Luther vigorously asserted the limits to human reason in understanding God. Luther's attitude toward reason is one that needs to be heard today. Today, as then, the temptation is great to demand a rigorous internal logic to faith that quite simply does not fit. Luther understood that there will always be an aspect to the life of faith that defies reason and often will simply not make sense. And students need to hear that today.

---

3. Becker, *The Foolishness of God*, 3.
4. Ibid., 4–5.
5. WA 8, 127, in ibid., 5.
6. WA 43, 240, in ibid., 42.

Luther and Reason

TODAY'S INTELLECTUAL CONTEXT

One of my former youth group students, who often came to our high school Sunday school class, posted recently on Facebook a short quasi-poem for Easter:

> This is Thomas.
> Thomas was into critical thinking before it was cool.
> Thomas demands evidence for supernatural claims.
> Be like Thomas.
> Happy Easter, everyone

This particular student came from an intelligent, high-achieving family, and he kept his faith for a long time despite his older brother's turn to atheism. He is now a young man, graduated from college, working, and finding his way in the world. His thoughts, expressed in this brief poem, I believe are representative for many students today.

First, he was right: critical thinking is "cool" today. This student likely believed that faith was easy or natural in the past, and that critical thinking was something new and original to our time. This is, of course, not the case. Nearly one-hundred years ago, Max Weber said, "The fate of our times is characterized by rationalization and intellectualization and, above all, by the 'disenchantment of the world.'"[7] This disenchantment of the world is pervasive today and is no longer novel. It means that faith cannot be taken for granted, and must stake its claims against a secularism that seems to be the rising default mode of belief in Western cultures.

---

7. Gerth and Mills, *From Max Weber*, 155.

LUTHER, REASON, AND FAITH

Is it any wonder then, that my former student's cry for evidence and that faith make sense is one that resonates with me on a deep level as well as many students with whom I have worked? But Luther would have had harsh things to say to any Christian who tried to reason like that. "It is the very nature of reason, says Luther, to judge only by what it sees. In this it is diametrically opposed to faith, for faith judges by what it does not see . . . Human reason cannot go beyond judging by what it sees with its eyes, or feels, or grasps by the senses. Faith, however, judges independently of and even against the data furnished by the senses and clings only to what is offered in the Word."[8]

This type of thinking is as offensive to the many highly rational people who have rejected faith today, just as it would have been in Luther or St. Paul's day. Luther declares that faith, "follows nothing but the bare Word, even if it is contrary to all sense and contends against all human reason, yes, against its own senses and everything that it sees, feels, and hears."[9]

The demand for supernatural evidence that my former student spoke of is not unreasonable. It makes a lot of sense. Yet, it is completely at odds with what Luther would say it means to live as a Christian. Luther calls to mind stories from the Bible to illustrate this point, such as Abraham's faith that he would have a child in his old age, or Noah's faith to build an ark despite those who doubted him.[10]

---

8. Becker, *The Foolishness of God*, 100.
9. WA 24, 173, in ibid., 101.
10. Ibid., 100–101.

Luther and Reason

Today, students regularly look for evidence or experiences to validate their young faith. Perhaps this is natural and developmental, something to be judged lightly and looked upon with grace. However, Luther would counsel that, just as confusion, doubt, and bad experiences are not sufficient to argue against God's existence, so too good experiences and answered prayers do not argue for God's existence.[11]

This can be a helpful reminder for students who are hungry for validation of their faith. They will likely encounter just as many times when their prayers seemingly go unanswered, with God frustratingly silent, as when they feel a strong sense of God's presence and that God has answered their prayers. The teeter-totter existence of judging from the vicissitudes of life can be overcome by realizing that God's presence in our lives can't be bound up in our good and bad experiences, but instead can be seen through trusting God's promises.

Luther even held that these difficult experiences in life were necessary conditions for the life of faith to emerge: "Reason follows only what it can see. But it must be put to death, so that the Word and faith may have a place. However, reason cannot be put to death, except through despair, mistrust, hatred, and murmuring against God, so that at length, when all external objects have been removed, the soul may cling to and rest in only the Word and sacraments."[12]

Luther's approach to understanding God's puzzling work through difficulties in life could be summarized this way:

---

11. Ibid., 102–3.
12. WA 43, 395, in ibid., 104.

> In this way the children of God learn to know that God is nearest just at the moment when he seems to be farthest away. At the time when he seems to be most angry, when he sends them afflictions and trials, they know him best as their merciful Savior. When they feel the terrors of sin and death most deeply, then they know best that they have eternal righteousness. And just when they are of all men the most miserable they know that they are lords over all things.[13]

Luther held that human reason was always limited in its ability to grasp the things of God because of its fallen and distorted nature, and its tendency to turn particular events into universal truths.[14]

One tendency today, in the face of attacks by those calling for Christianity to show evidence, proof, and reason, is to do our best to force it to make sense to modern people, and remove the scandal, rough edges, and the seeming impossibility of faith. The Christian life is then reduced to rote spiritual practices, legalistic moralisms, and sermons on "Five Ways to Fix Your Marriage." Children's and youth workers can especially fall prey to these tendencies as we have to translate a difficult message into bite sized pieces that make sense to our students.

Against these tendencies, Luther reminds us that according to human reason, God tells us: "Impossible things, lies, foolish things, weak things, absurdities, abomination, heresies and diabolical things! . . . It is always the case that when God sets articles of faith before us, he conveys to us things that are simply impossible and absurd—if you want to follow the judgement of reason."[15]

13. WA 36, 494, in ibid., 105.
14. Ibid., 106–7.
15. WA 40, 1, 361 in ibid., 108.

Luther and Reason

Among those things that seem ridiculous, Luther lists the Lord's Supper, baptism, the resurrection of the dead, the virgin birth, and Jesus's shameful death on the cross.[16] Without faith, God's promises simply do not make sense according to reason, no matter how palatable we attempt to make them. "Thus reason is the greatest hindrance to faith, because it deems the things of God to be absurd nonsense."[17] "Reason sees that the Word defies all understanding, that it is against every sense, feeling, and experience. So reason falls away from the Word of God or denies it completely or, if it cannot avoid it, turns and twists that Word with comments until it finally agrees with reason. But then faith has no more place. Faith has to give way and concede the victory to reason."[18]

That is what eventually happened with my former student who posted the poem on Facebook, and likely many others as well. For him, faith lost when Christianity was tried at the bar of reason and found wanting. I wonder if I could have done a better job as a youth worker to help such students. We often tried to puzzle and reason through some of the great and difficult aspects of faith during our high school Sunday school classes. We were never afraid to wade into the most difficult of intellectual issues, and I thoroughly enjoyed the many questions that the students had.

And yet, in retrospect, I wonder if trying to reason through these issues together set us up for misplaced expectations in the life of faith. Perhaps I tried too hard to present a version of Christianity that could make sense if a person puzzled over and studied it enough, without ever

---

16. WA 40, 1, 361 in ibid., 116.
17. TR 3, 62 in ibid., 111.
18. WA 36, 493–94, in ibid.

acknowledging the inherent unreasonableness of the life of faith.

If a student leaves our ministry in high school believing that Christianity was meant to make sense and conform to reason, then we have truly failed in our jobs as youth workers. Faith and God's promises simply do not make sense according to our reason. Attempts to reconcile them will only lead to the triumph of reason and the loss of faith.

YOUTH MINISTRY TODAY

So, if Luther is correct, how can we practice ministry with children and youth today in a culture which views a project such as this as utter, contemptable foolishness? Luther's use of paradox certainly does not alleviate the difficulty of explaining the unreasonable life of faith to children and youth. However, it does open up the possibility for imagination as one considers the seemingly contradictory and opposite ways in which God works:

> Faith has to do with things not seen. In order therefore that there might be a place for faith it is necessary that all the things which are believed should be hidden. However, they are hidden no farther away then [sic] under the opposite object, feeling or experience. Thus God, when he makes alive, does this by putting to death; when he justifies, he does this by making guilty; when he takes to heaven, he does this by leading into hell.[19]

These seemingly silly contradictions could be a good way to open for children and youth the paradoxes of the

19. WA 18, 633, in ibid., 125.

Luther and Reason

life of faith. How is it that it is necessary that "all things which are believed should be hidden?" Or that God makes alive by putting to death? Questions like these could begin to give children and youth an introduction into what it means to go beyond reason into the life of faith.

Luther's concept of the hidden God may also be a fruitful one in explaining the strange ways of faith to children and youth. Luther held that since the Fall, man can have no direct knowledge of God, and that it is impossible for man to know God in God's bare, divine majesty.[20] God is a hidden God, and cannot be found in our speculations, pictures, analogies, or senses of God. Thus, "Nothing is more dangerous . . . than to build one's own road to God and to climb up by our own speculations."[21] If we seek to understand God purely through our speculations, "the questions will multiply in direct proportion to the time spent on them, and there will be more questions than sand on the seashore."[22] So, "What God has revealed you cannot understand, even if you tear yourself to pieces over it. Therefore be on your guard against this very common temptation of wanting to know. "Why does God do this?" Friend, watch out for that "Why?" or you will break your neck . . . On this apple we all still choke."[23]

God does reveal Godself, but even in doing so, God remains hidden.[24] God comes to us in ordinary ways that reveal yet still conceal Godself, such as through a voice, a dove, the water of baptism, and the bread and wine of

20. Ibid., 13.
21. WA 42, 625, in ibid., 14.
22. WA 47, 545, in ibid., 15.
23. WA 47, 543–44, in ibid.
24. Ibid., 16.

the Lord's Supper.[25] Ultimately and most conclusively, we know God through Christ. "If men want to know what the will of God is concerning them, let them listen to Mary's Son. Outside of him God has locked up his heart and has hidden his will."[26]

THE PLACE OF REASON IN THE LIFE OF FAITH

According to Luther, reason is "a big red murderess, the devil's bride, a damned whore, a blind guide, [and] the enemy of faith."[27] However, Luther also considered reason to be "God's greatest and most important gift to man, of inestimable beauty and excellence, a glorious light, a most useful servant in theology, [and] something divine."[28] So, is there a place for reason in our life of faith? And, what are the limits of Luther's assault on reason? Despite his substantial and damning critiques of human reason, Luther clearly was not advocating for people to turn their brains off. Luther was one of the most brilliant and influential theologians in the history of the church who deeply valued both sacred and secular education, so Luther was clearly not instructing against the life of the mind: "insofar as it is the instrument which man uses to examine his environment, to interpret his experiences and to discourse about them, Luther valued reason highly."[29]

At this point I will go beyond Luther a bit and speculate on how we can use our minds today in fitting together

25. Ibid., 18.
26. WA 47, 540, in ibid., 20.
27. Ibid., 1.
28. Ibid.
29. Ibid., 69.

science and scripture, and the tricky aspects of biblical interpretation. I cannot, unfortunately, claim that I would have received Luther's blessing on my speculations here. It is simply my attempt to draw out Luther's insights on the limited nature of human reason along with the need for faith, but to also give credence to the difficult task of interpreting scripture in light of its scientific study and the scientific study of all that God created.

Luther never saw the day when the scriptures could be studied so scientifically. Textual variants, the knowledge of other languages and cultures of the Ancient Near East, and the many other apocryphal early Christian writings are just a small sample of the issues which Luther never faced in his study of scripture. Luther could recognize the difficulty of his position, but still hold to the historicity of the account of the origins of humanity and other contested scriptural accounts.

Likewise, Luther lived before Newton and Einstein, and never had to contend with the insights of archaeology, physics, or biology that threaten overly literal readings of scripture. So it is a bit unfair to expect of him answers in these arenas that would be beneficial for today. Even the concept of "adolescence" would have been foreign to Luther. So how can we appropriate Luther's insights for today?

First, we can value Luther's high estimation of reason for discovering truths about the natural world. Just as Luther valued and promoted education, so should we. We have nothing to fear from the discoveries of science if we trust in the promises of God. We may at times struggle in confusion in darkness, but God has not left us bereft, but has given us his Word and his promises. All truth is God's truth—wherever it may be found.

Second, we must also remember Luther's vehement admonitions against using reason as a way to reach God, or to understand God in God's bare majesty. No matter how much we reason, think, and try to put together the mysteries of faith, we will never reach God with them, and ultimately must contend with the hiddenness of God. God refuses to be found or tamed by our speculations, as well-intentioned as they may be.

As a final thought, as well as appropriating Luther's theology for today, we also must be cautious with aspects of it. Luther speaks strangely of God's hiddenness in *The Bondage of the Will*, seemingly going beyond his own injunction against speculating about what God is like apart from God's revealed word. Luther also held that we have no basis for judging the morality of God's actions, and that whatever God decides to do is good by definition, no matter whether it seems evil or immoral to us.[30] This coincides with his judgment of the twisted nature of human reason, but it leaves us little to go on if we cannot adequately judge whether or not an action is moral or immoral, whether it be for God or anyone else.

Yet, I believe that ultimately Luther's insights are crucial correctives for how children and youth perceive the world today. Althaus explains just how revolutionary Luther's thinking should be to Christians:

> All this makes clear that the theology of the cross results in a new understanding of what we call "reality." True reality is not what the world and reason think it is. The true reality of God and of his salvation is "paradoxical" and hidden under its opposite. Reason is able neither to understand nor to experience it. Judged by the standards of reason and experience, that is

30. Ibid., 144.

> by the standards of the world, true reality is unreal and its exact opposite is real. Only faith can comprehend that true and paradoxical reality.[31]

Luther's thought points to the necessity of faith in the life of the believer. This should be obvious to anyone who is a Christian, but it is all too easily overlooked in a culture in which Christianity can easily be called to account for not conforming to the strictures of reason and logic. Paul Althaus describes the dilemma in which we find ourselves: "To believe means to live in constant contradiction of empirical reality and to trust one's self to that which is hidden. Faith must endure being contradicted by reason and experience; and it must break through the reality of this world by fixing its sights on the word of promise."[32]

The good news for my former students is that faith, as a work of God, can exist even when it appears to be gone. "Our capacity to believe is so minimally involved that faith is not always aware of its own existence. Luther can even say that someone who is certain that he believes does not believe at all while someone else who seems to be completely bogged down in doubt and despair really believes most strongly."[33] I know that I have seen times like that in my own life as well. Also, "Someone admittedly may neither wish nor be able to speak of his own believing; he may even feel that he has no faith. Still he can bear witness to the power of the word of truth which does not let him go and which repeatedly overcomes his doubt."[34] Finally:

> We are to believe not only because nothing else remains for sinners but because God is God and

---

31. Althaus, *Theology of Martin Luther*, 32.
32. Ibid., 33.
33. Ibid., 60.
34. Ibid.

man cannot honor him as God in any other way than by believing—because faith is the fulfilment of the First Commandment. Faith is the only attitude of man which corresponds to God's nature, God's deity. God's true godliness consists in the fact that he is the creator and that he creates out of nothing and even out of its opposite. Faith corresponds exactly to this. Faith expects something from God where nothing can be seen; it waits expectantly against all appearance. God's deity and man's faith correspond. Faith is completely directed to God as God; one can only completely believe and trust in him who is essentially God. Again, man cannot grasp, recognize, and honor God as God in any other way than with faith alone. Faith alone truly obeys and worships God as he really is.[35]

---

35. Ibid., 127–28.

5

Conclusion

What would it look like to carry Luther's reforming spirit into the future? For a long time, I thought a local megachurch pastor who led a large, multi-site church in the city where I live truly embodied Luther's reforming spirit. He was bright, charismatic, and controversial. He attracted large crowds of people wherever he went, and he was unafraid to make bold and provocative statements. This was similar to Luther, but Luther was aware of his own limitations in this respect: "[Luther's] negative judgements were never exaggerated; the two unfavorable qualities he emphasized in himself were confirmed by his contemporaries: extreme irascibility and verbosity. He found an 'official' excuse for his excess verbiage in his Saxon lack of breeding and thick-headedness."[1] Like Luther, this pastor was a fiery, passionate man, who often saw issues in black and white terms. Certainty about a cause has both benefits and liabilities: "Historians will admit that only an

---

1. Oberman, *Luther*, 298.

'Evangelist' who firmly knew himself to be on Christ's side could have given the Reformation its thrust. But where resistance to the Papal State, fanaticism, and Judaism turns into the collective vilification of papists, Anabaptists, and Jews, the fatal point has been reached where the discovery of the Devil's power becomes a liability and a danger."[2]

Perhaps a certainty and strong belief about the worth of one's cause is necessary for a reforming movement. What interested me about this pastor, compared with Luther as a great reformer of the church, is the eventual demise of the pastor's once large church. Plagued by charges of misogynistic statements, consolidating power for his own benefit, and uncaring, authoritarian leadership, the church eventually closed and the pastor moved to another community to start over again.

Given the clear gifts of each of these individuals, their capacity to communicate and inspire others, and their commitment to their causes, what led to one becoming a central figure in a reform movement that changed the Church and the other to resign and move away? I realized from this question that I had been misguided about why, exactly, Luther became a central figure in the Reformation.

First, I had gotten hung up on considering the personality and gifts of Luther, without realizing the most important part of the equation: the cause that Luther stood for and was willing to risk his life for. At its core, Luther's cause involved a new and revolutionary way to view scripture and the authority of the church, but it also reached into many other areas of life: marriage and family, faith formation, education, the role of the church in society, the role of the State, and much more. Luther's cause was broad

2. Ibid., 303.

Conclusion

and far-reaching, and involved a transformation of society, and eventually, Western culture.

The local pastor's appropriation of the Reformation, along with some of the gifts and personality of Luther, was primarily involved with conserving the past. He brought no new or novel way of approaching scripture, let alone any of the many areas that the Luther's thought reached into. Instead, this pastor focused on what conserving the past would look like in the present, both in theological and cultural arenas.

As we consider what it means to live into Luther's reforming spirit, this is an important distinction. Not all reformers today need to share Luther's forceful, passionate, and unique personality. They don't necessarily need to live up to his certainty about his cause or even his ability to communicate and inspire others. What we do need to do is to have Luther's ability to see problems in the church and society and be able to respond to them. While perhaps we can't be as clear as Luther was on who his friends were and who his enemies were, we certainly must be willing to act and stand for ways to repair broken systems and stand up for victims of injustice.

So what can be gleaned from Luther's practices with children and youth in a larger sense? Narrow results have been considered in each of the chapters, but I think there is a larger lesson that can be drawn from Luther's practices.

One conclusion that can be drawn from this look at Luther's life is a broadening of the scope of what churches are about in their care for children and youth. Luther had his greatest emphasis on the faith formation of children and youth, but his care for them did not end there. It extended into areas that are seldom considered by churches today: public education and orphan care.

Luther's work with children and youth calls us to look outward, beyond our families and beyond our churches, and out into what God is doing in the lives of children and youth in the community. Luther's work shows that God is concerned not simply for what the lives of children and youth are like in our churches, but there must also be an imagination for God's wider work in redeeming and restoring lives and broken systems in our culture and world.

If Luther had seen the ravages of poverty or racism in a multicultural society, no doubt he would have addressed those issues among youth as well. Luther's life calls us to think more broadly about our role as Christians and as churches. Luther's care for children and youth demands a larger scope that also addresses the difficulty of faith in today's rational culture. It calls us to take seriously the challenges wrought by scientific advances, and also to remember that faith cannot be manufactured or made to fit in a rational box. Let us trust in the gifts and promises of God as we discern the leading of God's Spirit in our work with children and youth.

Bibliography

Althaus, Paul. *The Ethics of Martin Luther*. Translated by Robert C. Schultz. Philadelphia: Fortress, 1972.

———. *The Theology of Martin Luther*. Translated by Robert C. Schultz. Philadelphia: Fortress, 1966.

"America's Changing Religious Landscape." *Pew Research Center*, 2015. http://www.pewforum.org/2015/05/12/americas-changing-religious-landscape/.

Anderson, Monica. "Men Catch up with Women on Overall Social Media Use." *Pew Research Center*, 2015. http://www.pewresearch.org/fact-tank/2015/08/28/men-catch-up-with-women-on-overall-social-media-use/.

Arand, Charles P. *That I May Be His Own: An Overview of Luther's Catechisms*. St. Louis: Concordia, 2000.

Aries, Philippe. *Centuries of Childhood: A Social History of Family Life*. New York: Vintage, 1962.

"Attendance at Religious Services by Metro Area." *Pew Research Center*, 2015. http://www.pewforum.org/religious-landscape-study/compare/attendance-at-religious-services/by/metro-area/.

Bainton, Roland H. *Women of the Reformation in Germany and Italy*. Minneapolis: Augsburg, 1971.

"Be Undivided." http://beundivided.com/.

Becker, Siegbert W. *The Foolishness of God: The Place of Reason in the Theology of Martin Luther*. Second. Milwaukee: Northwestern, 1999.

Boswell, John. *The Kindness of Strangers: The Abandonment of Children in Western Europe from Late Antiquity to the Renaissance*. New York: Pan-theon, 1988.

Bruce, Gustav Marius. *Luther as an Educator*. Minneapolis: Augsburg, 1928.

Bibliography

Central Lutheran Church. "Welcome to On the Corner!" Accessed October 26, 2015. http://www.clcyakima.org/otcclc.html.

CityServe Portland. "History," 2013. http://cityservepdx.org/schools/community-connections-2.

———. "School Partnership Network Reaches Significant Milestone," 2013. http://cityservepdx.org/happenings/item/school-partnership-network-reaches-significant-mileston.

Dean, Kenda Creasy. *Almost Christian: What the Faith of Our Teenagers Is Telling the American Church*. New York: Oxford University Press, 2010.

Everist, Norma Cook. "Luther on Education: Implications for Today." *Currents in Theology and Mission* 12 (1985) 76–89.

Fischer, Robert H., ed. *Luther's Works*. Vol. 37. Philadelphia: Fortress, 1961.

Forde, Gerhard O. *Where God Meets Man: Luther's Down-to-Earth Approach to the Gospel*. Minneapolis: Augsburg, 1972.

Friedman, Thomas L. *The World Is Flat: A Brief History of the Twenty-First Century*. 3rd ed. New York: Picador, 2007.

Gerth, H. H., and C. Wright Mills, eds. *From Max Weber: Essays in Sociology*. New York: Oxford University Press, 1946.

Gilgoff, Dan. "Evangelical Minister Jim Wallis Is in Demand in Obama's Washington." *U.S. News and World Report*, 2009. http://www.usnews.com/news/religion/articles/2009/03/31/evangelical-minister-jim-wallis-is-in-demand-in-obamas-washington.

Godin, Seth. *Tribes: We Need You to Lead Us*. New York: Portfolio, 2008.

Harrington, Joel F. *The Unwanted Child: The Fate of Foundlings, Orphans, and Juvenile Criminals in Early Modern Germany*. Chicago: The University of Chicago Press, 2009.

KIDS COUNT data Center. "Children 0 to 17 in Foster Care." http://datacenter.kidscount.org/data/tables/6242-children-0-to-17-in-foster-care?loc=1&loct=2#detailed/1/any/false/869,36,868,867,133/any/ 12985,12986.

Kittelson, James M. *Luther the Reformer: The Story of the Man and His Career*. Minneapolis: Fortress, 2003.

Koestlin, Julius. *Life of Luther*. Translated by John G. Morris. Philadelphia: Lutheran Publication Society, 1883.

Kolb, Robert. "The Layman's Bible: The Use of Luther's Catechisms in the German Late Reformation." In *Luther's Catechisms—450 Years: Essays Commemorating the Small and Large Catechisms of Dr. Martin Luther*, edited by David P. Scaer and Robert D. Preus,

Bibliography

16–26. Fort Wayne, Indiana: Concordia Theological Seminary Press, 1979.

Kroker, Ernst. *The Mother of the Reformation: The Amazing Life and Story of Katharine Luther*. St. Louis: Concordia, 2013.

Lee, Morgan. "Common Core Meets VBS." *Christianity Today*, 2015. http://www.christianitytoday.com/ct/2015/august-web-only/vbs-common-core.html.

Light up the City. "LUTC Quarterly Gathering Recap." Accessed June 5, 2016. http://www.lightupthecity.org/#!LUTC-Quarterly-Gathering-Recap/e01rz/57438f9d0cf2a098d6143655.

Love and Logic Institute, Inc. "Love and Logic." https://www.loveandlogic.com.

Luther, Martin. "A Sermon on the Estate of Marriage (1519)." In *Martin Luther's Basic Theological Writings*, edited by Timothy F. Lull and William R. Russell, 3rd ed. Minneapolis: Fortress, 2012.

Martin, Sam. *Undivided*. Lightening Strikes Entertainment, 2013.

Martinson, Roland, et al. *The Spirit and Culture of Youth Ministry: Leading Congregations Toward Exemplary Youth Ministry*. St. Paul: EYM, 2010.

McLaughlin, Mary Martin. "Survivors and Surrogates." In *The History of Childhood*, edited by Lloyd DeMause, 101–81. New York: Psychohistory Press, 1974.

Miller, Timothy S. *The Orphans of Byzantium: Child Welfare in the Christian Empire*. Washington, DC: Catholic University of America Press, 2003.

"National Church Adopt-A-School Initiative." http://churchadoptaschool.org/.

Oberman, Heiko A. *Luther: Man Between God and the Devil*. New Haven: Yale University Press, 1989.

Painter, F. V. N., and Martin Luther. *Luther on Education: Including a Historical Introduction and a Translation of the Reformer's Two Most Important Educational Treatises*. Philadelphia: Lutheran Publication Society, 1889.

Root, Andrew. *Bonhoeffer as Youth Worker: A Theological Vision for Discipleship and Life Together*. Grand Rapids: Baker Academic, 2014.

Safe Families for Children. "Safe Families for Children." http://safe-families.org.

Search Institute. "Developmental Assets: Preparing Young People for Success." http://www.search-institute.org/what-we-study/developmental-assets.

Bibliography

Smith, Christian, and Melinda Lundquist Denton. *Soul Searching: The Religious and Spiritual Lives of American Teenagers.* New York: Oxford University Press, 2005.

Smith, Preserved. *Luther's Table Talk: A Critical Study.* New York: Columbia University Press, 1907.

———. *The Life and Letters of Martin Luther.* Boston: Houghton Mifflin, 1911.

Strauss, Gerald. *Luther's House of Learning: Indoctrination of the Young in the German Reformation.* Baltimore: Johns Hopkins University Press, 1978.

———. "The Social Function of Schools in the Lutheran Reformation in Germany." *History of Education Quarterly* 28.2 (1988) 191–206.

The Turn Around Agenda. "Public Schools Outreach (PSO)." http://www.turnaroundagenda.org/publicschoolsoutreach.

Wengert, Timothy J. *Martin Luther's Catechisms: Forming the Faith.* Minneapolis: Fortress, 2009.

www.ingramcontent.com/pod-product-compliance
Lightning Source LLC
Chambersburg PA
CBHW070517090426
42735CB00012B/2816